# Lord Nuffield

## 1877–1963

*An illustrated life of William Richard Morris,*
*Viscount Nuffield*

Peter Hull

*Lord Nuffield in the office at Cowley which he occupied for fifty years until his death in 1963. The office still remains, preserved exactly as it was when he was using it.*

# Contents

Cover image: A personal shot of Lord Nuffield, labelled 'sailing to Australia', *c*.1930s. Courtesy of the Heritage Motor Centre, Gaydon.

ACKNOWLEDGEMENTS
The publishers acknowledge with gratitude the assistance of Jim Bateman, former Chairman of the Friends of Nuffield Place, in the preparation of the second edition of this book, and also for the photographs on pages 5 and 14.

*Published in 2013 by Shire Publications Ltd, Midland House, West Way, Botley, Oxford OX2 0PH, United Kingdom.*
*© 1977 by British Leyland Ltd, 1993 by British Motor Industry Heritage Trust. First published 1977. Second edition 1993. Reprinted 2013.*

*A CIP catalogue record for this book is available from the British Library.*
*Shire Library no. 509. ISBN-13: 978 0 74780 203 7.*

Printed in China through Worldprint Ltd.

# Nuffield Place

In 1932 Lord and Lady Nuffield bought a house at Huntercombe, near the village of Nuffield in Oxfordshire, but did not move in until 1933, after having a number of additions and alterations carried out. The house had been designed and built in 1913 under the supervision of Oswald Partridge Milne, a pupil of Sir Edwin Lutyens, for Sir John and Lady Wimble; Sir John was in shipping insurance in the City. The house was called Merrow Mount and a ship's bell carrying this name survives at the back.

The house was built originally in the Lutyens style of architecture and, despite the additions, this is still discernible. Lord Nuffield did not employ an architect for the alterations but, characteristically, talked over what he wanted with the builder and left him to carry on with the work. When this was completed, the house, renamed Nuffield Place, had an enlarged sitting room and dining room, a new billiards room and kitchen and a closed-in upstairs veranda, which made a superb sun room.

The house was furnished mainly with very high-quality reproduction furniture commissioned by Lady Nuffield from the firm of Cecil A. Halliday of Oxford. There were also tapestries from the firm of Arthur H. Lee of Birkenhead and a collection of fine oriental rugs. Lord Nuffield's main passion in domestic furnishing seems to have been for clocks and there are several longcase, wall and mantle clocks around the house.

The house was decorated in the 1930s style and a great deal of the decor survives. There are textured wall finishes produced from mica-filled plaster and ragwork decoration in the study and Lord Nuffield's bedroom.

Lady Nuffield was a keen gardener. The garden of Nuffield Place had been designed by Milne during and just after the First World War. From 1933 it was tended by three gardeners, whose weekly wage bill came to £6. Now it is all done by one man!

An interesting feature which intrigues visitors to the house is the cupboard in Lord Nuffield's bedroom. It looks like an ordinary pine wardrobe, but it opens out to reveal a built-in workshop complete with bench, vice and a range of tools. It is said that when Lord Nuffield had difficulty in sleeping he tinkered around repairing clocks, mending shoes and doing other odd jobs — he was ever the mechanic.

Before Lord Nuffield died, he agreed with the late Sir Norman Chester, then Warden of Nuffield College, Oxford, that he would bequeath Nuffield Place to the College. After taking over the house in 1963, the College added a wing to be used by a curator appointed to look after the building and to comply with Lord Nuffield's wish that it should be preserved as it had been during his lifetime. Eventually this post disappeared, but now a group of Friends of Nuffield Place helps to fulfil this role and also administers open days for the public on the second and fourth Sundays of each month between May and September.

*Nuffield Place.*

*(Right) William Morris as a young man.*

*(Below) Twenty 'bullnose' Morris Oxfords lined up in Hollow Way, Cowley, in 1913. It was claimed that this represented a week's production.*

# The man who put Oxford on wheels

## LORD NUFFIELD'S OFFICE

William Richard Morris, Lord Nuffield, occupied the same office in his motorcar manufacturing works at Cowley, on the outskirts of Oxford, for fifty years until his death, aged eighty-six, in 1963. A small green-painted room in a converted nineteenth-century school building, it has been preserved more or less by accident exactly as it was when Morris was using it. Hardly the sort of room most people would expect a multi-millionaire industrialist to operate from, it does nevertheless provide a few clues to Morris's character.

It is perhaps surprising that no photographs or drawings of cars are to be found anywhere in the room. In the adjacent office there are car pictures, and there are also pictures of Morris himself, but none are in his own office. It is known he possessed a silver replica of a Morris Cowley car, presented to him by agents for Morris Cars in 1923. A similar silver model of an M type MG Midget was presented to him some years later by Cecil Kimber, as was a silver Morris 1000, but only a china bullnose souvenir and an MG model are in his office today. There are, however, two aeroplane models. One, which stands on top of the safe, is of Amy Johnson's Gipsy Moth biplane *Jason* in which she flew solo to Australia in 1930. A similar, or perhaps the same, model was attached to the radiator cap of the 18/80 MG coupe which Morris presented to Amy Johnson in recognition of her great flight. The second model, on the other side of the room, is of the Heston Type 5 Racer, a wooden single-seater monoplane powered by one 2,300-horsepower derated Napier Sabre engine and designed for an attempt on the world's air speed record in 1939-40. Two such aeroplanes were to have been built by the Heston Aircraft Co Ltd, the cost of £16,000 being met by Lord Nuffield, but only one was completed and registered to D. Napier & Son Ltd. This made one five-minute flight on 12th June 1940, piloted by Squadron Leader G. L. G. Richmond, when it was damaged beyond repair in a forced landing with an overheated engine and inadequate elevator control. Because of the war the whole project was then abandoned, yet Nuffield, evidently, did not choose to forget it.

Another thing he did not choose to forget was his career as a racing cyclist, for on the wall above the fireplace is a large cabinet containing innumerable small medals won by Morris in his late teens and early twenties when he was cycling champion of Oxfordshire, Buckinghamshire and Berkshire. An incident in his cycling career provides an illustration of his determination.

When he retired from competitive cycling in 1901, at the age of twenty-four, he had won the Oxford City one-mile title and the Oxford County fifteen-mile title for two successive years, 1899 and 1900. Had he won them for a third time he would have kept them for good, but a third event was not held until 1903, when Morris was asked to return the cups so that others could compete for them.

To the organisers' surprise, Morris decided to come out of retirement and defend his titles, which he did, after regular nightly training, with success at the university running grounds, Iffley Road, winning both the one-mile and fifteen-mile races, the latter through sheer stamina as all his rivals dropped behind and then gave up. Morris never raced a bicycle again.

On the same shelf as the model of the Heston Racer are tins of pills and Morris's sovereign remedy for most ailments — bicarbonate of soda. As befits someone who in his youth wanted to train as a doctor, Morris was intensely interested in medical complaints and their cure, both his own and other people's, and he was a great taker of pills.

His love of Oxford is shown by a painting of Magdalen Bridge which hangs above his desk, and an interest in meteorology seems to be indicated by three barometers, a hygrometer, a thermometer and a wind-direction indicator by the door. One barometer was won at deck tennis, and another was a present from his workpeople. (Other gifts from his workpeople were the hundred thousandth engine made at his Coventry engine factory, and a 25-horsepower Wolseley coupe.) That he was no lover of change is indicated by a defunct Ericsson telephone installed in 1913, a McMichael radio of the early 1930s and an air conditioning unit installed in 1937.

A final clue to his character is a framed copy of Kipling's poem *If*, also by the door, whilst on his desk, amongst a small pile of books,

*William Morris as cycling champion in the 1890s.*

including a dictionary and an introduction to pharmacy, is a copy of *The Imitation of Christ,* written about 1427 by Thomas à Kempis, a book praising the life of Christian service to one's fellows. The presence of this book might be less of a surprise to those who knew Lord Nuffield as a philanthropist than to those who sometimes found him something of a despot in his role as an employer.

## MORRIS'S EARLY LIFE

Morris was born on 10th October 1877 in Worcester, but both his parents, and indeed his ancestors, came from Oxfordshire, and his parents returned to Oxford around 1880. His father, Frederick Morris, had been a mail-coach driver in Canada in his youth, having sought his fortune in the USA and Canada after leaving grammar school, but returned home and in 1876 married Emily Pether, whose father farmed at Headington, Oxford. Frederick Morris became a bailiff on his father-in-law's farm, but attacks of asthma then forced him to take clerical jobs to support a family of seven, of whom William was the eldest.

William (or Will as he was called) was educated at the Church School at Cowley, leaving there at the age of fourteen to become apprenticed to a bicycle repairer, for he had already shown exceptional talent in dismantling things and putting them back together again.

## HIS OWN BUSINESS

It took young Morris only nine months to realise that he could make far more money by working for himself, and so, with a capital of £4, he set up his own bicycle-repair business in a shed at the back of his parents' home in James Street, Cowley St John, Oxford. This was in 1892, and one of the front rooms of his parents' house became his showroom and shop.

It was not long before Morris was building bicycles, the first one to the order of Mr Pilcher, Rector of St Clement's church, who was a large man and therefore specified a special 27-inch frame. This bicycle is still preserved by British Leyland.

Morris soon showed an infinite capacity for hard work and a tremendous energy, which distinguished him all his life, and by 1901 his business had expanded to take over premises for the sale of what were described as 'the celebrated Morris cycles' at 48 High Street, Oxford, which Morris himself once described as 'the most beautiful street in the world'. Further small premises were taken for cycle storage

*The first bicycle built by William Morris, with a special 27-inch frame.*

and repairs round the corner at 1 Queen's Lane, and a contract was obtained for the repair of the cycles used by the Oxford Post Office telegraph boys.

In 1900 Morris purchased the castings for a 1¾-horsepower engine, which he machined and built up himself and put into a frame to form his first experimental motorcycle. Within the next eighteen months he had decided to manufacture motorcycles to special order, having designed a machine around a 2¾-horsepower de Dion engine. These motorcycles rather resembled some of the mopeds of today, being heavyweight cycles propelled by a small engine.

At this time Morris took into partnership a cycling friend of his called Joseph Cooper, but the partnership did not last long, as Cooper became nervous about the resources being spent on the motorcycles when the cycle side of the business was so successful in itself. Morris had to repay Cooper his capital and lost a working partner, so he had a few problems, particularly as additional premises had now been taken

11

*William Morris began making bicycles at his parents' home but in 1901 moved his premises to 48 High Street, Oxford.*

at 100 Holywell Street, on the corner of Longwall. These were part of some extensive livery stables, always referred to as the Longwall premises, backing on to the city wall encircling New College gardens.

Morris always remained friendly with Cooper, who later returned to work on the first Morris car and finished up in charge of the Axle Department of the Nuffield Organisation. 'He could be where I am, but he did not take his chance', Lord Nuffield used to say of Joe Cooper.

Towards the end of 1902 Alfred Keen joined the business as a boy apprentice; he was destined to retire as a director of the newly formed British Motor Corporation in 1953. At the time Morris's father, Frederick Morris, who kept immaculate accounts, looked after 48 High Street, in the shadow of Oriel and Brasenose Colleges, a man and a boy looked after the storage, cleaning and small repairs of undergraduates' bicycles at 1 Queen's Lane, whilst Morris himself worked at Longwall with one other man and Alfred Keen, the boy apprentice. The employees often used to wear white woollen jerseys with *RIDE MORRIS CYCLES* embroidered back and front in red.

MOTORCAR REPAIRS

Soon the Longwall establishment was beginning to garage cars, often belonging to wealthy undergraduates, and by 1903 Morris was advertising 'Motor repairs a speciality'.

One of these undergraduates, who owned a Gardner-Serpollet steam car, inherited a large sum of money, and Morris formed another partnership with this undergraduate and an Oxford businessman dealing in cycles and cars, with three shops in Oxford, another in Abingdon and a fifth in Bicester. Morris was the only technical man of the three, and the Oxford Automobile and Cycle Agency was formed, with Morris as the works manager, repairing and servicing cars and making motorcycles in a workshop in New Road, neither Longwall nor 48 High Street being used by the Agency.

At first all went well, and then it was found that the undergraduate, although ostensibly a sleeping partner, was spending too freely in seeking new sales customers, and after little more than a year the Agency was wound up, the sale of its assets paying for its debts. Morris salvaged his tools and his business reputation was unharmed, so he went back to 48 High Street and Longwall, vowing to avoid partnerships in the future.

On 9th April 1904, at the age of twenty-six, Morris married Elizabeth Anstey, the daughter of an Oxford furrier, and they first set up house across the road from the old James Street workshop, which was still apparently in use, whilst Morris's parents moved to Argyle Street. His mother continued to live there until her death in 1934, aged eighty-four; her husband died at the beginning of 1916.

Before her marriage Elizabeth Anstey had been a schoolteacher. Except that she was retiring by nature, little is known about Morris's wife, who died in 1959 as Lady Nuffield, although she was said to be good at gardening and golf, was fond of animals but disapproved of drinking, and practised economies in the home even as a millionaire's wife. P.W.S. Andrews and Elizabeth Brunner in their *The Life of Lord Nuffield*, written during Lady Nuffield's lifetime, say she was a skilled driver, but Robert Jackson in *The Nuffield Story*, written after her death, says that she was so reckless that she once overturned her Morris Isis in the main road outside the drive of Huntercombe Golf Club because she was going too fast. Although her husband enjoyed a social drink in the evening, particularly a gin and French, it is unlikely that he offended her feelings about the consumption of alcohol.

In 1905 Morris began hiring out cars and drivers and driving tuition

*Elizabeth Anstey, who married Morris in 1904, was a schoolteacher. She died, as Lady Nuffield, in 1959.*

*Morris established a garage at Longwall, Oxford, for the repair of motorcars.*

was also given. He became agent for Arrol-Johnston, Belsize, Humber, Hupmobile, Singer, Standard and Wolseley cars, and for Douglas, Enfield, Sunbeam and Triumph motorcycles.

Something of Morris's mechanical skill and determination is illustrated by his experience in delivering a Lacoste & Battmann car from Paris to a customer in Stirlingshire, Scotland. He set out from Paris on New Year's Day, 1906. After twenty-five miles the transmission seized due to lack of oil in the back axle, and Morris returned to Paris for a spare part, which he fitted himself after working all night. Another start was made on 2nd January, but at midnight at Amiens an exhaust valve broke. A spare valve Morris carried proved to be too long, so he laboriously ground down the stem on a cobblestone. Once across the Channel the car broke down again after a few miles and was towed to Oxford, where new teeth had to be welded on to the gears. On 6th January Alf Keen and another driver set off for Scotland, only to break down at York that night with a broken bevel gear in the back axle. Morris then travelled up to York from Oxford by train, made and brazed on two new teeth in a blacksmith's shop and travelled on the car for the rest of the trip. At Berwick-on-Tweed there was more transmission trouble at midnight, where repairs were made on the road in freezing darkness. At last the car was driven into the customer's drive, where the transmission broke once again.

It seems that Morris preferred working on cars to driving them, as he did not take so much interest in racing as did his near contemporaries Herbert Austin and W. O. Bentley. He said that a racing programme invariably led to economic disaster. Nevertheless he later drove his Morris cars in sporting events and it could be argued that he did it mainly for advertising purposes, but there is evidence in 1908 that he took part in two speed hill climbs purely for the sport. On 29th February 1908 he drove one of his open Enfield hire cars in a University Hill Climb at Dashwood Hill, near High Wycombe, and made the fastest time, it is said, by not wasting time with unnecessary gear changes as did his undergraduate rivals. On 18th July 1908 he again made the fastest time of the day at the Oxford & District Automobile Club's Irondown Hill Climb, held on the Deddington-Chipping Norton road. He took 55.9 seconds to cover the 678 yards, driving a 40-horsepower De Dietrich.

## THE MORRIS GARAGES

By this time the cycle and motorcycle manufacturing part of the business had receded. In 1908, 48 High Street, the centre of the cycle business, was disposed of, and in 1910 the Oxford directory listed W. R. Morris as a motorcar engineer and agent and garage proprietor and no longer as a motorcycle maker. In 1907 some extra space in the yard of the Longwall garage became available, and as the old small wooden buildings were no longer suitable for the expanding business, they were pulled down and a completely new garage was built, completed in 1910. More premises were taken on in nearby St Cross Road and 'The Morris Garage' became the registered name of the business. Then, in 1913, after new showrooms were acquired at 36 and 37 Queen Street, the name was changed to 'The Morris Garages (W. R. Morris, Proprietor)'. In 1914 a further large garage was added in the Clarendon Hotel Yard in Cornmarket.

In 1913 William Morris brought his will to bear on the life of the city of Oxford. At the beginning of the century public transport in Oxford was provided, rather unsatisfactorily even at that time, by horse-drawn trams, and in 1902 there was pressure on the city council to replace

## WAKING UP OLD OXFORD.

# THE MODERN St. GEORGE AND THE DRAGON.

*A cartoon celebrating the conflict that Morris had with Oxford Corporation over the establishment of a motor bus service in the city.*

*One of Morris's motor buses alongside one of the horse-drawn trams with which he was competing.*

them by electric trams. Ten years went by and Oxford still had horse-drawn trams, when other cities of similar size had electric trams or motor buses. Morris was aware that the general feeling in Oxford was that motor buses would be preferable to electric trams, and he applied to the council for a licence to operate motor buses. His application was ignored, as the council was under an obligation to the owners of the horse trams.

Morris thereupon brought six Daimler buses and their drivers overnight from London and began to operate them the following morning. As he knew it would be illegal to collect fares on them, he arranged the sale of tickets in the form of coupons at shops on the first bus route from Cowley to Oxford station. The buses were an immediate success with everybody but the council and the horse-tram operators. The council sought ways to frustrate Morris, but without success, and finally started up a fleet of their own buses, only to find that the people of Oxford preferred to continue to patronise Morris's buses. In the end the controversy ended rather tamely when Morris finally sold his bus fleet to the council — but he had made his point.

# The birth of the Morris car

Throughout his life Morris was noted for his cheerfulness and energy. He was also a keen businessman and it has been said that he got the Post Office contract for repairing the telegraph boys' bicycles not because of his pleasant smile but because his price was less than anyone else's. As an employer he expected a fair return for the wages he paid, and in the early days at Longwall was affectionately known as 'Uncle' by his little band of employees. There is no doubt he could inspire loyalty in those working under him, and although he could be explosive at times he had a reputation for fairness and for not bearing a grudge against an individual employee once the explosion was over. In later years he showed that he trusted the judgement of his chosen executives and would even allow them their mistakes. On the other hand, there is evidence that he was capable of bearing grudges against institutions. It took him many years to forgive Oxford City Council for their behaviour over the motor bus affair, and he was no lover of the university after the unfortunate experience of the partnership with the undergraduate, so that for a long time he would not knowingly employ a university graduate, maintaining that they were useless in business. Eventually, after twice refusing it, he accepted the Freedom of Oxford from a city council of which not one single member was on the council at the time of the motor bus controversy, and in later life he became an enormous benefactor to Oxford University.

In appearance, Morris was slightly under average height and had very blue eyes. He hated 'dressing up' and even when he was rich his suits often looked as if they did not quite fit him.

Although an expert mechanic and an astute businessman, Morris was not an engineer in the design sense. He was not familiar with reading blueprints when he contemplated building his first car, and it is said he never took the trouble to learn how to use a slide-rule.

Morris knew what he wanted the Morris car to be like — a small

*The fleet of hire cars outside the new Longwall premises that Morris built.*

economical car of the highest possible quality for the price to be produced in quantity — and he realised he could produce what was required by buying the components at a keen price from outside firms and assembling the cars in Oxford.

### THE FIRST MORRIS CAR

By 1910 he had the finance to go ahead with the initial work at Longwall. The two-seater Morris Oxford was announced at the 1912 Motor Show and the car first appeared in March 1913.

Much of the credit for the design of the Morris Oxford must go to the firm of White & Poppe in Coventry, who were most famous for their carburettors, although they also were proprietary engine manufacturers of fairly big engines on a large scale. For Morris they specially designed and built a small 10-horsepower (8.9 horsepower RAC rating) four-cylinder side-valve T-head engine, with a 60mm bore and 90mm stroke, splash lubricated, with a three-bearing crankshaft and on which both the inlet and exhaust manifolds were cast with the cylinders. It is said to have been inspired by the design of the much larger engine fitted to the Italian Itala car of Prince Borghese which won the extraordinary Peking-Paris race in 1907.

White & Poppe also designed and made the three-speed gearbox and multi-plate clutch and naturally a White & Poppe carburettor was used. Hans Landstad, a young Norwegian, was White & Poppe's chief draughtsman, and, besides being responsible for the engine and gearbox design, he also drew out the chassis for Morris. The transmission was enclosed in a torque tube with a worm-drive back axle, the axles and some other parts being made by E. C. Wrigley & Co of Birmingham. Sankey supplied the artillery wheels, Powell and Hanmer the acetylene headlamps and paraffin side and tail lamps, whilst the only foreign component was the German Bosch magneto. The bodies were made by the coachbuilding firm of Raworth, in Oxford, which many years later in 1944 became part of the Morris organisation.

Morris estimated he would sell 1500 Morris Oxfords and told White & Poppe to anticipate supplying fifty engines a week in due course — before he had even booked an order for a single car. Morris's personality and the fact that part of his finance had come from the Earl of Macclesfield persuaded P. A. Poppe to take on his business, Macclesfield having known Morris when he was up at Oxford ten years before. Peter Poppe was a distinguished Danish engineer, and the late Laurence Pomeroy once told a story about him to illustrate the difference between the engineer-mechanic of 1903, as epitomised by Morris, and the designer-engineer of 1913 as epitomised by Poppe himself.

In 1913 Poppe owned a 35-horsepower Lancia, and one day whilst he was driving Pomeroy's father, the famous Vauxhall designer, the engine stopped firing. Young Pomeroy immediately diagnosed that the timing had slipped and suggested how they should repair it, but the older Poppe remained adamantly at the wheel and lit his pipe saying 'No, no, dis is where we schmoke our pipes; dat is job for de mechanic, not for de expert'.

Although Morris was not able to get a car ready for the 1912 Motor Show and could only show the blueprints for it there and announce the specification, a London dealer, Gordon Stewart, was sufficiently impressed to order four hundred of the cars and pay a deposit on them. He made his fortune when his firm of Stewart & Ardern held the London distributorship for Morris cars in the ensuing decades.

When the Morris Oxford was first seen by the public its most

*A 1913 bullnose Morris tourer. This was Morris's first production model.*

distinctive feature was its bullet-nosed radiator, designed by Morris, which became famous as the 'bullnose'. The car was priced at £175, complete and ready for the road with all accessories, and out of this Morris had to pay White & Poppe £50 for the engine and gearbox. The car was made so precisely that no keys or keyways were used except to fix the flywheel to the crankshaft; otherwise castellations only were employed.

### THE WORKS AT COWLEY

The Longwall premises were not big enough for the production Morris visualised, so he bought some property at Temple Cowley, including the buildings of what had been Hurst's Grammar School, where his father had been educated. The school had been transformed into a military training college and considerably enlarged. Although when Morris bought them the buildings had not been used for twenty-one years (and their value had therefore depreciated), the military buildings were ideal for the factory and the school buildings for the offices. In addition Morris also bought the attractive Temple Cowley

Manor House nearby, where he lived with his wife and was very close to the works.

Morris formed a new company, registered in August 1912, for the manufacture of the cars. It was called WRM Motors Ltd, and he was managing director and the Earl of Macclesfield was president. Morris Garages Ltd carried on as a separate concern. 393 Oxfords were sold in

*A brochure issued by WRM Motors Ltd in 1913/14 advertising the Morris Oxford at £175.*

10 h.p. 4-cylinder Morris-Oxford Light Car.

50 Miles to the Gallon. Price £175. 50 Miles per Hour.

DETAILED SPECIFICATION

ENGINE.
GEAR BOX.
CLUTCH.
LUBRICATION.
RADIATOR.
IGNITION.
CARBURETTOR.
CONTROL.
FRAME.
CHASSIS.
FRONT AXLE.
REAR AXLE.
BEARINGS.
STEERING.
BRAKES.
SUSPENSION.
WHEELS.

1913 through ninety-nine agents in London and the provinces, and 909 in 1914, when Morris had agents in Holland, Belgium, Denmark, Italy, Scandinavia and Uganda. The price in 1914 went up to 190 guineas. On the original car there was only room for tools and luggage behind the two seats, but minor modifications were made for 1914/16 such as fitting a slightly bigger radiator and lengthening the wheelbase by 4 inches to allow for a dickey seat. Cooling was by the thermo-siphon principle with no water pump. Production life of the model, which was advertised as being capable of 55 miles per hour and 50 miles to the gallon, was from March 1913 to March 1917, and a total of 1475 cars was built.

In June 1913 Morris entered a hill climb on the Mountain Road at Caerphilly, and his 10-horsepower Morris Oxford was described as being 'rather slow', although a 10-horsepower Bugatti was not much faster. His class, which was run on formula, was won by an 11.9-horsepower Arrol-Johnston. In the Motor Cycling Club's London-Edinburgh trial at Whitsun 1914 five Morrises were entered and all won gold medals, including a coupe driven by W. R. Morris himself. Finally on 29th August 1914, when Britain was already at war, the Coventry & Warwickshire Motor Club held a hill climb for motorcycles and light cars on the 1 in 8 Style Kop. Out of nearly a hundred entries, there were only four in the light car and cyclecar class, and of these W. R. Morris's lone Morris Oxford was best both on time and formula

## THE MORRIS COWLEY

Sales of the Morris Oxford were restricted because it was only a two-seater, and Morris's intention was to produce another model beside it with a more powerful engine to which it would be possible to fit four-seater as well as two-seater bodywork; this was to be called the Morris Cowley.

He inquired of various firms about supplying parts for a second model; they seemed doubtful that they could provide the parts in the quantities Morris envisaged. White & Poppe were working to capacity and could not make the larger engine required.

Thus, early in 1914, Morris made his first visit to America, with a twofold purpose to find out something about American mass-production methods, and to see if it was possible to acquire parts for his new car from the USA. This was probably the first of the many sea voyages Morris made. He thoroughly enjoyed this method of travel, for

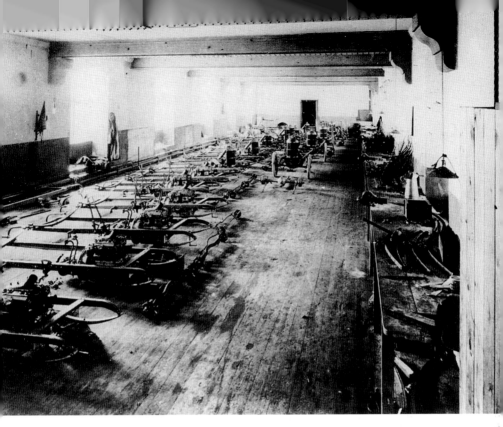

*Production of the Morris Oxford in the old military school at Cowley.*

he was a good sailor, and he became a tremendous expert at deck tennis.

Although Morris did not place any contracts in America during his visit, he obtained plans for an engine, axles, steering gear, etc, and was surprised to find the engine would cost him only £25. On his return he asked Poppe why he could not produce an engine for this price, and Poppe said that perhaps he could if he moved his works to Detroit. It was agreed that Landstad would take a six-month holiday to accompany Morris on another trip to the United States, where Landstad would stay to study American production methods and assist Morris with his planning of his new model.

They sailed in the *Mauretania* in April 1914, Morris travelling first class and Landstad, who was paying his own expenses, second class. Drawings of the proposed new model were made on the voyage until Landstad succumbed to seasickness. These drawings were continued in their hotel in Detroit, where Morris ordered three thousand 11.9-horsepower 1495 cc Type U Red Seal four-cylinder side-valve engines from the Continental Motor Manufacturing Co, an order which pleased the Continental Company as these engines were considered to be too small for the American market. Axles and steering components were also ordered, the rear axle having bevel drive, and a three-speed gearbox from the Detroit Gear Machine Co. In 1915 each engine was to cost Morris £17 14s 2d, and each gearbox £8 6s 6d.

After three weeks Morris returned to England, fortunately, due to a train delay, having cancelled his passage on the SS *Empress of Ireland,* which sank in a collision at the mouth of the St Lawrence river with the loss of all her passengers.

Landstad stayed behind, working with the Continental Company, and supervising the delivery of the parts Morris had ordered, but in December he returned to England, where he joined WRM Motors at Oxford and became Morris's chief designer.

The Morris Cowley was announced in 1915 as selling for 158 guineas as a two-seater, using the Oxford chassis, and 185 guineas as a four-seater on the new long chassis; this price included Lucas electric lighting, hood, screen and horn and a complete set of tools, at a time when such items often had to be bought as extras. But the First World War interfered with Morris's carmaking plans, for the first Continental engines were not delivered until September 1915, and about half the engines ordered were sunk by U-boats.

A few cars continued to be made, but the Cowley works were mainly occupied with the manufacture of munitions, firstly in machining the cases for bombs fired from Stokes trench howitzers, and then in manufacturing large numbers of mine sinkers, designed to touch the bottom of the ocean and pay out a length of wire hawser to keep the mine at a predetermined distance below the surface. Morris was glad to have Landstad as his chief designer to design the jigs and tools for their manufacture. At the end of the war Morris's supply of the sinkers had outstripped the demand, so greatly did he improve manufacturing methods, and he was awarded the OBE.

# Expansion and philanthropy

The strain of war work and setting up his factory affected the health of the normally fit Morris, and early in 1919, when he was forty-one, he spent six weeks at a German spa, the only place where he could get suitable treatment for what was thought at the time to be diabetes.

In July 1919 Morris Motors Ltd took over the assets of WRM Motors Ltd, which Morris had put into liquidation in order to free himself of certain agency contracts which he had entered into without realising their implications, an experience from which he learned a lesson.

The working space at Cowley was enlarged by a new steel building, which covered the old parade ground, and an assembly line was instituted along which the chassis were pushed, the line not being mechanised until the mid 1930s. Before the First World War the line had been stationary and the workers had moved along it to complete their tasks.

## A COMPLETELY BRITISH CAR

Once the American engines and accessories which had been stored during the war were used up, Morris was able to return to his aim of building a completely British car. The Continental engine was unsaleable in the USA and, as Morris had purchased the drawings and some of the tools to make them, he had to look for an engine manufacturer to produce his engines. White & Poppe were too busy with other contracts, but the work was undertaken by the French firm of Hotchkiss et Cie at their factory at Gosforth Street, Coventry. A peculiarity of these Continental engines made by Hotchkiss is that all the threads were in metric form and pitch, but the hexagons were Whitworth instead of metric to fit British spanners. Capacity was 69mm by 102mm, 1550cc.

Bodies of the Cowley cars were made by Hollick & Pratt of Coventry, who established a branch in Oxford under Mr L. W. Pratt for exclusive manufacture of bodies for Morris cars, although Raworths still made special bodywork. Radiators were made by Osberton Radiators, the Oxford branch of Doherty Motor Components of Coventry, in a disused skating rink in Osberton Road which had been taken over by Morris Motors. Chassis frames, which had at first been imported from Belgium, were made by Rubery Owen. Fisher & Ludlow made radiator shells, axle housings and other pressings, Ransome & Marles made ball bearings, Lucas supplied lighting equipment and Smiths the speedometers and clocks.

Morris sold 387 cars in 1919, of which only sixty-three were the new type Morris Cowleys. Only the new models were sold in 1920, and by April 140 cars a month were being sold, rising to 280 in July and September. In October 1920 a slump began to set in, and in January 1921 only seventy-four cars were sold when the factory was geared to producing a minimum of sixty cars a week. At the beginning of February, there was hardly room to park all the cars which had been produced, and something drastic had to be done. Morris did it by slashing up to £100 off the price of each model, the four-seater Morris Cowley going down by £100 from £525 to £425, and the two-seater by £90 from £465 to £375. The Morris Oxford name had been revived for a more luxurious version of the Cowley, and prices of Oxfords were reduced by £25 to £510 and £565 for the two-seater and four-seater models respectively, whilst the Morris Oxford coupe went down £80 to £595.

Even with these reductions, the profit was an average of £50 a car, and when sales dropped in 1921 from 351 cars in June to 172 in October, Morris made yet another price cut, this time up to £110 in the case of the four-seater Oxford, partly due to economies in production of bodies, which were built on a line system instead of each body being made individually.

Morris was confident that with the new prices he would double production and told his suppliers he expected to buy their parts cheaper if he ordered larger quantities. In fact he more than doubled production, selling 3076 cars in 1921 and 6956 in 1922. This increased rapidly to 20,048 in 1923 and 55,582 in 1925, by which time he had broken the monopoly of Ford with their Model T, which had been hit by an increase in horsepower tax to £24 a year. The smaller cylinder bore of the Morris meant that the Morris owner only paid £12 a year.

*The 'Doctors' Coupe' was a popular bullnose style.*

By this time Morris had standardised repair charges.

He installed printing presses at Cowley to produce the magazine *Morris Owner* under the editorship of the motoring journalist Miles Thomas, as well as printing instruction books, manuals and all other stationery requirements of Morris Motors Ltd on his own presses. A sad loss to Morris in 1924 was the early death of L. W. Pratt, at the age of forty-four. Originally of Hollick & Pratt, he had become a much valued second-in-command to Morris.

Useful publicity was provided for Morris in 1921 when John Prioleau, the motoring correspondent of the *Daily Mail*, wrote of his experiences touring France, Italy, Morocco, Algeria, Tunisia and Spain in a British car he named *Imshi*, which was afterwards revealed as being an 11.9-horsepower Morris Oxford two-seater. His adventures were later published in book form, and a second journey to southern and eastern Europe was undertaken in 1922 with a second *Imshi*, in this case a four-seater 11.9-horsepower Morris Oxford.

This free publicity delighted Morris, who would much rather spend money on improving his product than on advertising. In the *Autocar* of 15th October 1921 a Morris Motors advertisement was headlined 'NO MORRIS-COWLEY in the 200-Miles Light Car Race! Is this sporting

— is it wise?' After explaining how the 1922 buyer, and no one else, would pay for a Morris team in this race at Brooklands, the advertisement ended: 'As to the ADVERTISEMENT concerned and the EXPERIENCE gained, why, please remember that *Imshi* of the *Daily Mail* took a hundred times more strain than any 200-mile race could offer — *and the Daily Mail paid for it*. Put up a 200-mile race for models taken out of STOCK ONLY, and the Morris-Cowley is the first entrant'.

From 1921 until 1924 Alf Keen put up some sterling performances in sprints and hill climbs up and down the country in a sports Morris-Cowley he had specially tuned to be capable of 90 miles per hour and finally ran as a single-seater. Morrises proved to be quite formidable competitors in the MCC reliability trials of the day, and had they set their minds to it the works could no doubt have produced cars capable of putting up a meritorious performance in the 200 Miles Race. In the early days of the firm Morris always listed a sports model.

In 1923 the Oxford was given a bigger engine, with the cylinders bored out to 75 mm, giving a total capacity of 1800 cc, and the horsepower was increased to 13.9. The vintage bullnose cars were notable for having smooth cork-lined clutches running in oil, when many of their rivals had fierce cone clutches. They had very silent electric starting by means of a dynamotor and chain. Efficient front-wheel brakes were fitted in 1925 to the Oxford and were available at first as an optional extra on the Cowley.

## TAKEOVER OF SUPPLIERS

At this time Morris Motors was not a public company, as Morris preferred to risk his own money and not that of other people. In this way he was able to buy up the firms which were suppliers to Cowley if he felt that by doing so he could increase their efficiency. One of the first he took over was Osberton Radiators Ltd, which was his own property from 1923, but which he sold to Morris Motors in 1926 when the firm became the Radiators Branch. In a similar way Morris took over the Hotchkiss works in Coventry in 1923, having formed Morris Engines Ltd for this purpose, selling to Morris Motors in 1926 to form the Engines Branch. Hollick & Pratt, the Coventry bodybuilders, were also bought by Morris and sold to Morris Motors in 1926 to become the Bodies Branch.

*The Bullnose Morris at the height of its success. The advertisements on the wall publicise Morris's price war, which ruined his opposition.*

E. G. Wrigley & Co Ltd of Birmingham, which had supplied so many parts for the original Morris Oxford, was in liquidation in 1923, so Morris decided to expand his commercial-vehicle production and bought the Wrigley works in which to manufacture them, forming Morris Commercial Cars Ltd in February 1924. This company was not bought by Morris Motors until 1936.

Morris had always been interested in carburation. The story is told that he was working on a number of carburettors on a bench when the Earl of Macclesfield approached him and jokingly said: 'Why don't you leave that to somebody who knows something about it?' This nettled Morris and led him to send the Earl a cheque for £25,000 to buy him out of the business. Indeed Morris had soon realised that the Earl wanted more say in the running of the business and their association was quite short-lived.

Morris had been particularly impressed by the SU carburettor, but, 1922 models apart, he had not fitted it to his cars because of its high cost. In 1927 he bought the business, which had been formed by two inventor brothers called Skinner (their family was in the Lilley & Skinner shoe-manufacturing business) many years before, SU standing for 'Skinners' Union'. With Carl Skinner still in charge, under Morris's management the SU firm became a highly successful business and from the time of the takeover all Morris cars were fitted with SU carburettors.

In 1926 General Motors of Detroit offered Morris £11,000,000 for his business. Morris politely turned down the offer, telling Alfred Sloan Jr, the President of General Motors Corporation, that Morris Motors Ltd was not for sale, adding: 'Even if it were, it would not be for sale to an *American* firm'. Thus the General Motors share of the British market had to be through their acquisition of the Vauxhall company.

In 1927 the famous old firm of Wolseley Motors went bankrupt, and as its name and goodwill were obviously valuable there were three main bidders for it, William Morris, Herbert Austin and General Motors of America. In the early years of the century Herbert Austin had been Wolseley's chief designer until his resignation to start his own company, so he had sentimental reasons for being a bidder. It is said that many years before Morris had applied for the Oxford agency for Wolseley and the Wolseley executive had refused to see him. Although he later got the agency, the refusal to see him had always rankled with Morris and gave him an incentive to want to be the owner of the firm twenty years later. Morris's bid was successful and he acquired the firm for £730,000. Afterwards he said: 'It was the most thrilling day of my life.'

## UNSUCCESSFUL PROJECTS

Wolseley Motors became yet another successful Morris company, but not all Morris's business projects were successful. One of the most disastrous was Morris Collieries Ltd, Morris's attempt to enter the coal industry by buying Howbeach Colliery in the Forest of Dean. The colliery turned out to be waterlogged and no amount of pumping would clear it, so that the business was wound up eighteen months after Morris took it over in 1927. For a long time nobody dared to mention the words 'coal mine' in Morris's presence.

Two unsuccessful models built by Morris were the F-type six-cylinder of the early 1920s, of which only about fifty were sold, and later a four-cylinder Colonial model produced by Morris Commercial

*Lord Nuffield in old age, with an early Wolseley and a Cowley-built Wolseley. He paid £730,000 for Wolseley Motors when the firm went bankrupt in 1927.*

in 1927 for overseas use only. Far more disastrous, though, was his attempt to manufacture a Morris car in France by taking over the Leon Bollee factory at Le Mans in December 1924 and forming the Societe Francaise des Automobiles Morris Leon Bollee. Bollee himself had been a pioneer manufacturer and built engines for the Wright brothers' aeroplanes, and Morris bought his factory from his widow. At first a 12-horsepower four-cylinder car was made on the lines of the existing Leon Bollee car, but then an overhead camshaft straight eight was produced, with the engine owing much to Wolseley design. However, there were difficulties with the work people and with the suppliers. A very small number of straight eight cars was produced and the company was wound up and the assets sold in 1931.

The Morris-Bollee works were much used by the British and other teams in the Le Mans twenty-four hour races of the 1920s when they needed to make repairs or alterations to their cars during the practice

*Henry Ford on a visit to Cowley in 1928.*

period — something the patriotic Morris would have approved of if it aided a British victory.

A visit Morris paid to the United States in 1925 convinced him that mass-production car manufacturers were going to use pressed steel bodies in the future, and by an arrangement with the Budd Company of Philadelphia, who held the main patents, he formed the Pressed Steel Company in Oxford. His surmise was correct, but in order to gain the custom of other manufacturers it was later found advantageous to sever the link between Pressed Steel and Morris Motors, even though the latter was one of Pressed Steel's best customers.

A new company, Morris Motors (1926) Ltd, was formed in June of that year to acquire Morris Motors Ltd and the various subsidiary companies. Against City advice, Morris issued only cumulative preference shares, keeping £2,000,000 of ordinary shares to himself. The experts were confounded; the £3,000,000 issue was oversubscribed and Morris remained in full control.

The last bullnose Morris was produced in 1926, for in 1927 all Morrises had square radiators, and the Oxfords of 1927 and 1928 were the first British cars to have bodies made by the Pressed Steel Company.

## DIVERSIFICATION OF MODELS

The policy of Morris Motors to produce only one basic model had lasted a long time but was altered in the late 1920s, whilst in the 1930s the firm could be criticised for producing too many different models. The acquisition of Wolseley brought some changes in engine design, for since they had manufactured Hispano-Suiza aero engines during the First World War, known as Wolseley Vipers, Wolseley had been advocates of the overhead camshaft engine, which was more complicated and expensive to produce than the side-valve engines Morris had always used but had a greater power potential. The big 2½-litre Morris Isis of 1930 showed much Wolseley influence with its six-cylinder overhead camshaft engine and Pressed Steel bodywork, the latter also showing marked American influence in what was a good-looking car with a distinctive radiator shape. The Morris Oxford Six, on the other hand, which came out in 1929, had a side-valve engine fitted with a 'fume-consumer head', which was an air cleaner resembling a camshaft cover on top of the cylinder head, so that the uninitiated could easily assume that the car's simple side-valve engine was an overhead camshaft unit.

The most important aspect of the influence of Wolseley overhead camshaft design was that it virtually bred the famous line of MG cars, a make which became world-famous.

In the later 1920s Morris was anxious to provide a challenge to Austin's famous Baby Austin, which had held a unique place in the affections of the public since its introduction in 1922, when it rendered obsolete the chain-driven cyclecars, with air-cooled motorcycle engines. The Austin Seven had been designed as a unique entity with an emphasis on light weight and a tiny engine, whereas Morris's Morris Minor was merely a scaled-down large car with an 847cc overhead camshaft engine, slightly larger in capacity than the side-valve Austin Seven unit, in a heavier conventional chassis. It was therefore not such

35

*A 1925 MG sports tourer, evolved from the Morris Oxford and Morris Cowley. The initials MG stood for Morris Garages, and the vehicles were originally produced at the Longwall premises.*

a clever design as the Austin Seven, and its engine was unnecessarily complicated for what it had to do. In the early 1930s this engine was replaced in the Morris Minor by a simpler side-valve unit which was more satisfactory and powered the celebrated £100 Morris Minor.

The overhead camshaft Morris Minor had been chosen by Cecil Kimber as the basis of a new MG model called the MG Midget. Kimber had been appointed by Morris as manager of Morris Garages in 1922. He soon began to produce hotted-up versions of Morris cars with special bodywork, which were called MGs — standing for Morris Garages. So successful were these cars, originally produced at the Morris Garages premises at Longwall, that eventually, in 1927, a new factory was built in Edmund Road, Cowley, to produce them. Soon the biggest MG, the 18/80, had a six-cylinder overhead camshaft engine developed from the Morris Isis unit, but its chassis was more MG than Morris. The little Minor-based Midget was an immediate success, and in 1930 a large new MG factory outside Oxford, at Abingdon, came into use, and the Midget and the models developed from it, in particular the six-cylinder Magnette, had many racing successes. Some special racing cars were built, culminating in the independently sprung

R-type single-seater, although after 1935 the MG Company was evidently forced to acknowledge the Morris dictum about racing bringing about bankruptcy. They stopped entering works teams, though they did give support to private owners. Morris, in his turn, acknowledged interest in the sport by presenting the Nuffield Trophy for competition in a race at Donington Park, the first of the series in 1934 being the first long-distance road race ever held in England, run over one hundred miles. The distance was increased year by year, until in 1939 it was doubled.

## MORRIS IS ENNOBLED

In 1929 Morris was created a baronet, and became Sir William Morris. In 1934 he was made a baron and in 1938 Viscount Nuffield of Nuffield in the County of Oxford, in recognition not only of his work as an industrialist but also as a benefactor to various causes, particularly in the medical field.

Indirectly it was an interest in golf which led him to choose the title

*Heavy vehicles were an important part of Morris's activities and in the 1930s Morris was the largest-scale commercial-vehicle builder in Europe. Here Morris studies a bus chassis.*

of Lord Nuffield. He began playing golf in his early thirties, and his favourite course was Huntercombe, near Henley-on-Thames. This was a fairly exclusive club and in 1926 it got into financial difficulties, so Morris bought it. For the second half of his life, Huntercombe became a second home for Nuffield, long after he had given up golf because of his sciatica. As he grew older, Nuffield suffered from aches and pains and also from sleeplessness, and he found he could sleep better in a flat at Huntercombe than he could at home at Cowley Manor. Later he built a cottage behind the golf club and then purchased a small manor house called Nuffield Place, in the village of Nuffield nearby, and it was from the name of this village that he took his title. Many of Lord Nuffield's doctor friends, particularly those from Guy's Hospital, were members at Huntercombe, and he enjoyed their company. Nuffield was not one of those millionaires who never carry money on them — his wallet was always full of £5 notes which he was ready to spend.

## BENEFACTIONS

Nuffield's first two benefactions were made in 1926 when he gave £10,000 to enable parents to visit their children in borstal institutions and another £10,000 to Oxford University to found the King Alfonso XIII Chair of Spanish Studies, as Morris (as he was then) was interested in the promotion of business with Spain and South America, at that time hindered by lack of knowledge of Spain and its language.

Early medical benefactions were to hospitals in Birmingham and Coventry, where Nuffield had factories, although £104,000 was given to St Thomas's Hospital in London in 1927 and 1928. His first gift to an Oxford hospital was in 1930 — £1,000 to the Wingfield Orthopaedic Hospital at Headington, where the surgeon, Professor G. R. Girdlestone, was doing marvellous work for crippled children. A further £70,000 in 1933 for rebuilding brought a change in the name to the Wingfield-Morris Hospital. More large donations in Oxford went to the celebrated old Radcliffe Infirmary, established at the end of the eighteenth century, in the building of a maternity home ('so that any woman in Oxford can have her baby in hospital', Nuffield said) in 1932 and the purchase of the adjacent old Observatory site in 1930. Part of this was used for research and postgraduate medical training under the Nuffield Institute of Medical Research, and the rest for extending the Radcliffe itself. Largely due to these enormous gifts, Oxford was

*Morris began to play golf in his early thirties. His favourite course was Huntercombe near Henley-on-Thames and he is pictured playing there in the Automobile Golfing Society's autumn meeting in 1933. He bought the golf club in 1926 after it had got into financial difficulties.*

changed from a university with little interest in the medical sciences to one that rivalled London in that field.

Guy's teaching hospital in London was another favourite charity, receiving gifts of nearly £168,000 between 1934 and 1938, and a statue of Lord Nuffield can be found in its grounds. Other hospitals in such places as Exeter, Worcester and Banbury benefited, besides institutions devoted to the alleviation of blindness and cancer.

Nuffield did not forget his employees, £2¼ million being put aside in 1936 for stock in Morris Motors, the dividends from which were paid to hourly workers in addition to their wages; the salaried staff benefited from a contributory pension scheme. Nuffield would never contribute to the cost of housing for his workpeople, saying that was the job of the Government, and he was probably unwilling to be accused of paternalism. Nuffield always said he was apolitical and had a typical industrialist's distrust of politicians, unlike Lord Austin who, for a time, was a Member of Parliament himself. Nuffield was a constant contributor between 1928 and 1948 to the funds of the Motor and Cycle Trades Benevolent Fund.

What were called 'Special Areas', places where unemployment was rife due to the slump of the 1930s, were of interest to him. The Nuffield Trust for Special Areas helped to set up or reconstitute industries in places like Tyneside, South Wales, west Cumbria and central Scotland. The collieries at Whitehaven in Cumbria, which had closed down in 1935, were reopened through the work of the Trust, and Lord Nuffield was given the Freedom of the Borough of Whitehaven in 1953. Between 1936 and 1953 he also acquired the Freedoms of Coventry, Worcester, Cardiff, Droitwich and Oxford.

His benefactions to Oxford University particularly helped the less well endowed colleges, and in various ways he helped St Peter's Hall, Worcester, Pembroke and Lincoln Colleges. In 1937 he gave £900,000 for the setting up of Nuffield College on a site between Worcester and Pembroke Colleges. He had originally purchased the ground with the intention of making the approach from the west towards the city centre as attractive as was that from the east over Magdalen Bridge. He had wanted this to be a college of engineering and commerce but the Oxford authorities did not wish to compete with Cambridge, which had long had extensive facilities for training engineers. This was a blow to Nuffield, but he agreed that Nuffield College should be devoted to postgraduate studies in the social sciences. The Second World War meant the plans for building the new college had to be deferred, the foundation stone not being laid until April 1949, but the work of the college went on during the war.

# War and loneliness

Morris Motors, like other manufacturers, were hit by the slump of 1930-1, and sales dropped from 63,522 in 1929 to 45,582 in 1931. They were strong enough to weather the storm, but it was not until 1934 that they regained the 1929 sales. All sizes of models were made from 8 to 25 horsepower, but perhaps the one most similar in character to the old Cowley was the Morris Eight. Many thousands were built in the four years from its introduction in 1934, and they successfully challenged the ubiquitous Austin Seven.

The engine was a developed and slightly bigger version of the old side-valve Minor engine and had been designed by Leonard Lord, a production engineer from the Hotchkiss factory.

Nuffield had been impressed by Lord's capabilities and he was transferred to Cowley where he was responsible for expanding the factory and putting in a mechanical conveyor line. He soon became Nuffield's right-hand man as managing director of Morris Motors. In 1936 Lord resigned (he was a forceful character — some said there was not room for two Lord Nuffields within the organisation) and he later went to Austin at Longbridge.

In 1938 Nuffield purchased Riley Motors of Coventry, designers of the engine which in developed supercharged form powered the ERA racing cars which won every one of the Nuffield Trophy races at Donington Park from 1934 to 1939. Victor Riley was managing director of his old firm and also had a seat on the board of Morris Motors.

## AIRCRAFT AND TANKS

Lord Nuffield was keen to enter the aviation industry and as early as 1929 an aero-engine department was established at Wolseleys, when that firm was privately owned by him. When Morris Motors took over

Wolseleys in the mid 1930s Wolseley Aero Engines Ltd was formed as a new private company still owned by Lord Nuffield.

The model aircraft in Nuffield's office might give the impression that he was fond of flying but when the writer contacted Mr M. N. Mavrogordato, who used to be the pilot of Lord Nuffield's Leopard Moth before the war, and told him about the preservation of the models, he said: 'I'm surprised. I don't remember him ever coming out to look at the aeroplane, and although I flew his secretary around a lot, I never took him up once!' Nuffield's interest in aeroplanes was seemingly strictly from the business and patriotic point of view, linked with the fact that he could foresee the outbreak of the war with Germany. But he did not receive support from the Air Minister and Wolseley Aero Engines closed down, so Nuffield did not participate before the war in the 'shadow factory' scheme as did most of the other large British motor manufacturers.

Instead he turned to tank manufacture for the War Office. At that time, before the Second World War, Russian tanks had a form of suspension which allowed them to travel fast over rough ground, suspension which was derived from that on a tank designed by an American engineer, Walter Christie, which the Americans themselves had not taken up. Nuffield was so impressed with this suspension design that in 1937 he invited Christie over from the USA to work on the design of the Cruiser tank. An interesting point in view of the advent after the war of the famous transverse-engined front-wheel-drive Mini (product of the British Motor Corporation, the merger between Morris and Austin) is that in the early years of the century Christie had been a front-wheel-drive pioneer in the USA, racing his big front-wheel-drive racing cars in the 1906 Vanderbilt Cup race on Long Island and in the 1907 French Grand Prix at Dieppe. Like the Mini of the future, Christie's racing cars, too, had transverse engines. There was no suitable engine available for the Cruiser tank, so designers of the newly formed Nuffield Mechanizations and Aero Ltd, situated next door to Wolseleys in Birmingham, produced an engine closely based on the old Liberty aero engines, originally products of the Ford Motor Company in the First World War. Later a Rolls-Royce engine was used in the larger Crusader tank. Nuffield Mechanizations also began manufacturing the Bofors gun in 1938, after a visit to Sweden in 1938 by Hans Landstad to study the manufacturing process.

Once war had broken out, the Nuffield organisation's contributions to the war effort were enormous and included the repair of warplanes at Cowley, where an airstrip was built, the manufacture of Tiger Moth trainers and Beaufighter and Lancaster power plants, besides Cruiser and Crusader tanks. Mine sinkers were also made there as they had been in the First World War. At Coventry and Birmingham engines were made for fire pumps, ambulances, lifeboats, tanks and aeroplanes of all kinds; Bren-gun carriers, a huge number of jerricans, parts for Horsa gliders and many types of aircraft carburettors were made at SU. Complete Spitfires were built at a factory at Castle Bromwich despite interference by the Ministry of Aircraft Production. The list is almost endless.

The war brought trades unionism into Nuffield factories for the first time as well as further benefactions from Nuffield himself for the benefit of the forces. His benefactions to other causes as well continued after the war, and in particular they helped children, old people and the disabled. Doctors themselves benefited by £250,000 given to the Royal College of Surgeons for a residential college.

## THE BRITISH MOTOR CORPORATION

In 1936 the engineer Alec Issigonis had left the Rootes Humber-Hillman Co to go to Cowley, where he was largely responsible for the Series M Morris Ten of 1938, the first Morris with chassis-less construction, and also the first Morris with a pushrod engine. After the war Issigonis designed the famous new Morris Minor, an excellent and highly successful car which it is said Nuffield never liked and used to ridicule. Later Issigonis designed the famous front-wheel-drive transverse-engine Mini and was knighted for his achievements.

In 1952, when Nuffield was seventy-five, the British Motor Corporation was formed by acquiring the share capital of Morris Motors and the Austin Motor Co. The merger was arranged by Lord Nuffield and his old associate Sir Leonard Lord (later Lord Lambury) of Austins, Austin himself having died in 1940. Nuffield was chairman for a brief six months, but then he retired and handed over to Lord.

In his retirement Nuffield lived a secluded existence at Nuffield Place, although, until he was eighty-three and no longer able to take the wheel of a car, he frequently drove the sixteen miles to his office at

Cowley to deal with invitations and correspondence in connection with his numerous charities. His car was a humble 1939 Wolseley Eight, a more expensive version of the M series Morris Eight. After he lost his wife in 1959 his life was even more lonely and in his last years he suffered three painful major operations. The end came for him on 22nd August 1963, after an illness which he fought with his usual tenacity, hovering between life and death for more than a fortnight.

## LORD NUFFIELD AS A MAN

In his lifetime Nuffield gave away over £30,000,000, and at one time in his career was said to be earning £2,000 a day. When asked about the benefits of riches he once said: 'Well, you can only wear one suit at a time.' He was very unwilling that his fortune should go in death duties, which he was obviously very successful in avoiding.

He did not have expensive tastes, except that latterly he smoked rather special cigarettes called 'Maryland, made especially for John Hollingsworth and Son', which his secretary during the last seventeen years of his life, Carl Kingerlee, once described as 'quite unsmokable'. Perhaps Nuffield's one luxury was the long sea voyages he was able to indulge in. They began in the winter of 1927-8 and continued regularly until shortly before his death, enabling him to indulge in his passion for deck tennis.

He has been accused of meanness because he complained that scraps of soap were being wasted in the works washroom basins, but this is something any executive might take note of and no more to be deprecated because this particular executive happened to be a millionaire. Nuffield hated waste, even to the extent of saving string and slitting open envelopes to use the insides for scribbling notes, a habit acquired in his youth which he never lost.

He appeared to have a mistrust of journalists and disliked them writing about him, nor would he allow any book to be written about him until he authorised a biography published in 1955. The two authors were primarily economists. An author who sent him the manuscript of a book about his life was threatened with a libel action. Nor was Nuffield keen to see pictures or statues of himself, although he did cooperate with Maurice Lambert, RA, when he sculpted the statue destined to be erected in the grounds of Guy's Hospital. Honours of all kinds were showered on him.

Nuffield, apparently, was a good mimic, and he did not lack

humour. He was capable of a good turn of phrase, although he did not relish public speaking. In 1945-6 he was in Australia and arranged to buy what he understood was the disused Victoria Park Racecourse in Sydney, in order to erect a body shop there. He was accused of interfering with horse racing, although he made the arrangement on the assumption that there was no prospect of racing ever taking place on the course again, and replied to his critics: 'I must confess that I know very little about horse racing, nor have I any profound understanding of the influence it exerts on the national advantage in the improvement of the horse as an animal'.

He was hardly a patron of the arts, his major contribution in this direction being £25,000 to the Kipling Memorial Fund in 1937. He liked a Gilbert and Sullivan tune, but had little other interest in music.

His secretary, Carl Kingerlee, said Nuffield was religious, and he certainly gave £36,000 for the building of St Luke's church, Cowley, in 1937. At this time his workpeople were pressing for a rise in wages which would have cost the company about this amount and which Nuffield refused as he said it could not be afforded. The discovery of the gift to the church was not taken very well by his dissatisfied employees.

Nuffield loved repairing mechanical things, whether they were cars, clocks or cigarette lighters, and spent much time in his workshop at Nuffield Place right up to his death. He had always been happy to stop and roll up his sleeves to go to the assistance of a motorist whose car had broken down.

In his will he disposed of a further sum in excess of £3,000,000, most of which, although bequeathed to Nuffield College, was lost in death duties. Personal legacies were few and small; £1,000 to his maid, £4,500 to a niece and £500 to Alf Keen, although his trustees said he had made many private gifts to people before he died. A nephew, a brother-in-law and a first cousin by marriage received nothing, and it is said this came as no surprise to them.

Morris always regretted that he did not have a son to carry on his title, and might have been saddened to know that, under British Leyland, production of Morris cars would cease in 1983, just twenty years after his death. Yet it seems likely that the many causes to which William Richard Morris, Viscount Nuffield, so freely contributed huge sums of money will still be benefiting men and women for many generations to come.

THE PRINCIPAL EVENTS OF LORD NUFFIELD'S LIFE

1877  10th October: William Richard Morris born at Worcester.
1880  His parents return to Oxford.
1891  Morris leaves school and is apprenticed to a bicycle repairer.
1892  Morris sets up his own bicycle repair business in Cowley.
1900  Morris builds his first motorcycle.
1901  Morris acquires 48 High Street, Oxford, for the sale of cycles.
1902  Alfred Keen joins him as an apprentice.
1903  Morris wins Oxfordshire, Buckinghamshire and Berkshire cycle races for third and last time. He advertises 'Motor repairs a speciality'.
1904  9th April: Morris marries Elizabeth Anstey.
1907  Expansion of the premises at Longwall.
1912  Morris forms WRM Motors Ltd for manufacture of cars.
1913  Morris opens new showrooms in Oxford and operates a motor bus service from Oxford to Cowley. The first Morris Oxford appears. Built in the new works at Temple Cowley.
1914  Morris twice visits USA and orders engines from Continental Motor Manufacturing Company.
1915  The Morris Cowley produced, but the works concentrate on war supplies.
1919  New Morris Cowley appears. Morris Motors Ltd takes over from WRM Motors Ltd.
1921  Morris reduces prices due to slump in sales. Production more than doubles each year to 1925.
1923  1800cc Morris Oxford produced.
1924  Morris Commercial Cars Ltd formed. Morris takes over Leon Bollee Factory at Le Mans.
1926  Morris Motors takes over several of its suppliers. Takeover bid by General Motors rejected. Morris's first benefactions.
1927  Morris purchases SU Carburettors and Wolseley Motors. Morris Oxfords produced with Pressed Steel bodies. MG factory built at Cowley.
1929  Morris becomes a baronet and the first Morris Minor is produced.
1930  MG factory built at Abingdon.
1934  Morris made a baron. First Nuffield Trophy race. Morris Eight introduced.

1936 Leonard Lord resigns as managing director of Morris Motors.
1937 Nuffield gives £900,000 to found Nuffield College, Oxford.
1938 Morris becomes Viscount Nuffield. He purchases Riley Motors.
1939 Second World War begins — Morris factories concentrate on the war effort.
1949 Foundation stone of Nuffield College laid.
1952 British Motor Corporation formed from Morris Motors and Austin Motor Co; Nuffield is first chairman, but resigns after six months.
1959 Death of Lady Nuffield.
1963 22nd August: Viscount Nuffield dies.

BIBLIOGRAPHY

Andrews, P. W. S., and Brunner, Elizabeth. *The Life of Lord Nuffield.* Basil Blackwell, Oxford, 1955.
Jackson, Robert. *The Nuffield Story.*   Frederick Muller Limited, 1964.
Jarman, L. P., and Barraclough, R. I. *The Bullnose and Flatnose Morris.* David and Charles, 1976.

# INDEX